No Walk In The Par
Stumbling Through Mot

A debut poetry collection by Jemma Chawla

Jemma originally comes from the north-east coast of England. She now lives in West London with her partner, who she met while studying at university "down south". They have two young children together.

Jemma began sharing her words when her eldest child started school in September 2020, mid pandemic. Finding herself in a daunting new space, she took to poetry as a means of processing some very raw emotions – and to help her adjust to a slightly emptier house.

Her work covers many topics, but this particular collection focuses on Jemma's journey through motherhood so far. From anxiety, depression, self-doubt, rage and loneliness to heart-warming nostalgia and moments of deep joy, Jemma channels the full spectrum of maternal emotion across various poetic forms.

She enjoys writing pieces that resonate with others, in the hope that readers feel a little less alone during the difficult times and a little more comfortable talking collectively (should they wish) about some otherwise stigmatised topics.

Jemma's writing has been featured by a range of anthologies and zines, as well as multiple websites and other award-winning online publications.

No Walk In The Park

Stumbling Through Motherhood

Contents

Hold On 13

Glow In The Dark 14

Trying 15

One Day At A Time 17

Mother Didn't Warn Me 18

That First Year 20

Home Is 22

Shoes 23

Lullaby 24

Mother's Love In Metaphors 25

i.   Motherhood Is… 26

Bubble 27

Wake Me 28

Tides Turn 29

Pancakes For Dinner 30

Cusp 31

Hallway Show 32

Soar 34

Correlation 35

To My Mother On My Birthday 36

Sleep 37

How Are You Really? 38

World Of Love, Ok Not THE World, But My World 41

Big Girls, Little Lies 43

Partners Prior To Parents 44

I've Just Had A Baby 45

Half Term 46

I'm Selling The Pram... 47

Stay At Home Mum 49

20/20 (Vision) 50

What Are You Wearing Around Your Neck? 51

Adulting 52

Footprints 54

Cancelled Due To Covid.. 55

Daddy And Me 56

RAGE 58

Kitchen Bangs.. 60

Trike To Bike 61

ii.   Motherhood Is… 62

Unearthed 63

Climb 64

Water 65

Cardboard Hearts... 66

New Kind Of Drunk... 67

Rainbows 68

Rookie 69

Of All The Things I Left Behind 70

Music Be Medicine 71

What's In A Name?.. 72

Wiping.. 73

Look Up 74

Mummified 75

This Way Friend 76

Rebuild Me 77

Guilt 78

Without Using The Word – Tell Me You're A Mother 79

Nostalgia Stage Call 80

Mother The Mother 82

Resolutions 83

iii.   Motherhood Is… 84

Cherish 85

Five 86

Ballerina 88

Treats 89

Me Time 90

You Are Enough 91

Guiding Hands 92

Out 93

iv.   Motherhood Is… 95

Silent Nights 96

Bond 97

Let Her Dream 98

Both Finally Asleep 99

Undone 100

ode to my notes app 101

More Than Mummy Mates 102

Pick A Number 103

For Sanjay, Zachary and Jessica – the heart behind all my words.

Dedicated to my Mum – new things can be daunting, but so very amazing too.

Hold On

At the edge of the pavement, "Wait, hold my hand!"
The internal alarm of fear rings loud,
Somewhat soothed by your small hand grasping mine.
The road provides me this cherished guarantee
that you still need me,
Or is it me clinging to you?
Ten fingers combined.
Squeeze…
You're oblivious to danger, cocooned in my grasp,
Guide you to safety, safe at last.
Eagerly anticipate the return journey –
Step
Pause
"Wait"
Pause
Hold my hand.

Glow In The Dark

Even before the hunger cries start,
new motherhood senses wake me.
Those floating few minutes to
ready and steady myself for you.

You're gazing up at me
With your kind brown eyes
Milk drunk chatters
New moon natters

Tiny tummy tremors cause your full-bodied hiccups.
I'll claim your windy smiles as if they were real ones.
Ideas and dreams shared, where you're my biggest fan.

Butterfly blinking signals your need for slumber –
But me, I'll stay up a little longer
to scrutinise your breathing;
Your rising and falling chest,
complete with back-of-hand breath check…
Your warm whispering wind gives me the satisfaction
I need to take rest.

Call me crazy, but I miss those sleep-deprived nights.
I miss the stillness of the sleeping house.
I miss the 3am sharp flick of a switch.
I miss the night-lamp's amber glow by my bedside.

So needy, so needed.

Trying

We started playing this game over dinner.
(I'll be honest, it was initially a distraction for me
removing tablet time from the table.)

I quickly unleash upbeat tones,
"Let's play, the amazing, the epic, drumroll please…
Things I love About You Game!"
I've seemingly applied enough drama, as they ask
what the rules are.

My son shoots his arm up, indicating he's having the
first go and reminding us he's the eldest of the two.
He starts: "Things I love about…" exaggerating and
prolonging the 'out' sound in the word 'about'.
He swings his pointed finger back and forth across
the table finally landing on me, "Mummy!" he yells.

He tells me how he loves it when I play superheroes
with him, especially when I set up goodies vs baddies
on the rug. When tiny Batman slid under the sofa,
and I conjured up enough energy (like the Hulk)
to lift it and he retrieved it using his wind-up torch,
"That's team-work hey Mum?"

He tells his sister she's great at dancing,
especially spinning.
She grins from ear to ear whilst twirling her pasta
and swinging her legs under the bench.

He thanks Daddy for post-bathtime tickle fights.
Dad looks over at me; I respond silently with an
endearing half-smile, chin and eyebrow shrug.

But today at dinner, I was exhausted and fed up with
the intensity of lockdown, exhaling, "I'm tired darling,
would you like to watch your tablet instead?"
(Crushing myself in feelings of failure as the words left
my mouth.)

"No Mummy, it's dinner time, I want to hear what
you love about me and I want to tell you all the things
I love about you."

I'm quickly reminded that I'm not the only one going
through a pandemic, and all of us need to be
comforted right now.

One Day At A Time

One day at a time
they said.
It will get easier
they said.
Words spoken with soft comfort
hit thunderously loud.
A deafening alarm reminding me
it must improve, I'll improve
But when?
Tomorrow?
Tomorrow's tomorrow?
Or perhaps it's the week after that…
Trapped in a perpetual countdown,
internal noise screams beneath
an external silence that smiles politely.
One day at a time
they said
Torture, with no end in sight.
I left unsaid.

Mother Didn't Warn Me

Like a herd of elephants,
my Mum used to say.
I can't quite believe it,
I now talk the same way.

She really didn't warn me.
She omitted important facts.
Now we're parenting blindly –
Is this how children act?

We play tiredness top trumps
and butt wipe roulette,
Go on quests for missing Hatchimals –
this one our favourite yet.

"I think she needs help!"
"Well she's shouting for you!"
Double the butt arguments,
when you give birth to two.

Gosh they follow me everywhere,
even to the loo.
I need contortion classes,
toddler beds aren't made for two.

Fussy eating stages,
Endless requests for a snack.
Stale-crisp-and-crumb flooring
in our family hatchback.

Your job now is Grandma,
fun days out at the park.
But I really needed forewarning
about that ruddy baby shark.

Mum, what did I do to you?
Was I a toddler sent from hell?
Could have done with these insights
on raising kids so well.

That First Year (after Karen McMillan)

We piled muslins high in squares of perfection,
laughing at how many we had been told to buy.
The balance soon to be knocked by a new reality,
and yes, we should have bought more.

We plonked you in the middle of the room and
just stared at you, no reaching for a TV remote,
we watched you endlessly emitting your own
addictive light.

"Put him down, you're making a rod for
your own back." My back, my rod, my baby.
I'm glad I held you, and boy you held me too.

I holidayed in the car, toured neighbouring towns
and drive-throughs, refuelling on silence, caffeine
and two-day-old text messages.

Intense worry was exhausting, my brain nor my
notes app could hold much more, I slipped in and
out of power-saving mode to survive –
and we survived.

Kind eyes, reassuring smiles and chats with
strangers, who just knew you needed them,
as they did too.

Afternoon naps, oh the naps! Where I ignored my to-do list; yes the house went neglected regularly, but you, never.

Ten months in, we told you, "You're going to be a big brother." So unaware, yet you smiled and still clapped on demand.

I stored that smile. My synapses flooded me with it whenever guilt would rise.

What a year...

The year two became three and then four.

Home Is

The house is the body, step inside.
Welcomed into a gallery of framed smiles
preserved behind protective glass.
Walls like arms hold up cherished faces,
both past and present.
My son's first footsteps lay forever
embossed on the living-room floor.
Windows like mirrors see past the glare, as
they project memories into the room; we reflect,
stay silent and hear the walls' nostalgic echoes
of my daughter's first words.
Six chairs, posture strong, backbone to gather –
Our table has soaked up more than spilt soup.
Wood swollen from tears of traumatic times,
stretched hands come together to smooth it out.
Upon it we've blown wishes into candles,
marking blessings of years shared.
The home is the heart, stay inside.

Shoes

School-run sling 'em on ones
Understated ankle-grazing ones
Painful blistering teetering ones
Fugly but oh-so-comfy ones
Open-toe pedicure pending ones
Puddle-jumping bright rubber ones
Should throw away but cling onto ones
Five sizes too big, take the bins out ones
Summer's finally here ones
Oops, borrowed and not returned ones
Winter wool-lined ones
Nostalgic nights, stubbed-out cigarette ones
Running, not far or fast ones
Flip flop – ouch! – toe stumping ones
But my favourite ones?
Not even my ones
Your tiny red first pair ones

Lullaby

Lull(ed with melody
once sung to me, now I sing
mother to b)**aby**

Illustrator – Rachel Dickens
@lollysnow

Mother's Love In Metaphors

Invisible. It birthed alongside you, an extra placenta;
nobody needed to check it, nobody else could see it,
but we could.

Fluid. Riding the ever-changing waves, clinging on,
learning with each new current, crashing into cliffs,
ready to repeat with the tide again and again.

Stretched. But just before it tears, folded back up,
tucked away to live alongside your collected coat
pocket treasures.

Bittersweet. Bite into a peach, not knowing how to
handle both sweet and sour at the same time, yet we
still swallow regardless.

Shared. Hand-me-down jumper, worn with love,
gifted with love – doesn't quite fit, so you mould
it yourself, turn up the sleeves and sow on some
extra buttons.

i. Motherhood Is…

my arnica lips healing bruised knees, and
kisses that soak up pain from grazed elbows,
way more effective than any first aid kit –
believing in the magic of you, like they do

Bubble

Everyone glares up in awe
at the twirling and whirling
Elegantly graceful as she rides the wind
I'm fortunate to know that her iridescent
beauty runs deeper than the surface
Gosh, look at her !
She wears the yellow sunshine so well
Free to twist and turn in the sky's blue hue
She soars higher

Me, I'm the rested bubble
I sit unnoticed, silent on the grass
But not green with envy
I'm just not yet brave enough to join my friend
I'll wait here and applaud her confident
sky-high performance

When it's time she won't forget me
We always leave together when we pop
She's asked if I want to ride with her next time
I'm not quite ready to go solo, so we start off as a
bubble within a bubble…

Dedicated to my dear friend Philippa, who encouraged me
endlessly, patiently waiting until I felt brave enough to step
forward and try something new – my bubble ride.

Wake Me

Wake me in the night
I whisper to the cold walls
I miss your warm breath

I wait in the dark
Strangely glad to hear you cry
Jump to be with you

Together again
Grateful, I rest next to your
little fussing legs

Tides Turn

Your birth –
autumn's welcomed
fall, descended into
unknown waters, sinking in red
rivers .

I wake –
helpless tides turn with bobbing hope
finally submerged in
calm seas as I
hold you .

Illustrator – Rebecca Green
@herworldofdiscovery

Pancakes For Dinner

The rain was due today. Instead, spring hinted at summer through the window – no tapping or waving, just invited itself right in, most welcome.

The noise, it too arrived, unexpectedly and most unwelcome. Not their noise no, that's a mild hum in comparison to this.

I cling to the kitchen counter, rage rising, bending at my middle like I'm bowing, succumbing to a stronger power. They notice it too; they turn and temporarily look at me slumped over in the sun's unforgiving spotlight.

I drop my chin to my chest trying to hide, from them, from it, from both. One deep cold breath…
…followed by five more that are suffocatingly hot, pulled through the threads of my jumper, my arms stretched out to support me, or were they extended, palms up begging for help?

As quick as the cloud came it passes over. I rise to announce, "It's pancakes for dinner!" They dance in delight at the announcement (the announcement I'll file under a feeding failure). I watch on; they continue chanting "pancakes" – still dancing in the sunbeams.

Rain was forecast today, and on these wet days it falls inside the house.

Cusp

You see evergreen
Exterior bright
Unfazed
Hardy roots
Beneath my virescent mask
I ache in this forested facade
Like broken bones, not visible
But it doesn't diminish the pain
Nor deny the snap
Weighed down
Just balancing
Somnambulant steps
Stumble on
I'm ready to be caught
Look at me
I'm on the cusp of roaring
When you first notice my decay

Hallway Show

Why do they do it?
Do they really scheme and plan?
8:15 I'm calm and ready,
Well that's quickly down the pan.

This is your five-minute warning!
I think that's when they know
I've alerted them, that now's the time
to start their hallway show.

Did you brush your teeth? Not yet why?!
They really take the mick.
Now your jumper's toothpaste-stained
and you sister claims she's sick.

Don't pull your hair out,
That's really most unhelpful.
Grab your book bag we have to go!
Why is leaving the house so stressful?

You'd never believe my pre-mummy job:
Department Project Lead,
forecasting and planning change –
Now can we leave on time I plead?

Where's your shoe? Find it NOW.
It's a new trick every morning.
Just pick a hat OH ANY HAT,
My organisation skills in mourning.

Can I bring a toy? Yeah, me too?!
Errr, well there really is no need.
But Mummy, Mummy, Mummy, Mum!
I shrug limply and concede.

Water bottles at the ready,
Face mask, bags, let's go!
Wait... I think I need the loo,
My school-run morning woe.

Soar

"Higher Mummy!"
Elevated exhilaration embraces a
welcome weightlessness.
"Send me to the Moon, Mummy!"
Searching for last night's sleeping stars
discovered dancing in her dream.
"Like a rocket Mummy!"
Little legs launch,
feet flapping fast in flight.
Whistling winds
whisper warm wishes…
She wails out a wondrous wake-me-up
"WHEEEEEEEEEEEEEE!"

Swinging in September's sailing sun,

                                        she soars.

Correlation

Two strangers collide and merge worlds.
From that day it was never questioned.
We just made space

for each other.

And
by
degrees
shaped the resulting us –

The us that would be tested, but not divided.

Our unit grew, now sharing love between two tiny
amalgamations of you and I.

=

We're not trying to calculate or prove the unique
formula; we just know it equates to what matters.

To My Mother On My Birthday

Thanks to her 21-year-old self
Her naive and not ready self
Her moved far away from home self
Her before she was a Mother self

Thanks to her pre-eclampsia recognising self
Her scared but put on a brave face self
Her lonely in a room full of strangers self
Her numb emergency c-section self

Thanks to her learning as she goes self
Her boundless love and get up every day self
Her nobody warned her self
All without her own Mother's calming hand self

A new overwhelmed self
A never experienced this self
Step forward but daunted self
A flooded with new love self

Happy Birthday – the delivery of a new born baby,
but also the birth of a Mother.

I see it now
Thank you Mum
For being your self
Love always, my self

Sleep

Sl(iver of the bed is what I'm left with, you call it sharing, too young for fractions just yet, let's carry on counting sh)**eep**

Illustrator – Debbie Brown

How Are You Really?

Nappy bags organised nightly – check
Two spare sets of baby grows – check
Add in an extra for my worry – yep

Buzzing with exhaustion but keep pushing through
Write countless notes describing your poo
First-time Mum this was all so new

Keep up-to-date don't miss an injection
Play dates planned with PA perfection
Got to keep busy make that connection

"You're doing so well"
"You're out every day"
I should have seen what was heading my way

Ten weeks in something stopped
My mask of organisation dropped
Pursuing a perfection bubble popped

I'd call Daddy at work and question my choices
He'd whisper back softly, no corporate sales voices

That day at baby yoga, I remember it well
She asked me a question and I instantly fell
Waved organised, structured and certainty farewell

"How are you…? How are you really?"

With nowhere left to hide
and no words to provide
Blinded by a blurry sea forming
I cried.

World Of Love, Ok Not THE World, But My World

It's Sunday morning, not sure of the time, until I get a text from Mum. 11:23am. Who knew doing not a lot (well apart from that, with him) would take up so much time. Her text message read: *Kids slept fine, don't know what you moan about. Jessie wants to make pizza so I'll bring them back after lunch. Love you Mum xx.*

The notification of more downtime instantly makes me giddy to change the trajectory. I'll wash my hair, cook, read and then write. Will I heck.

Instead, I do nothing.

It's a much-needed extension of this stillness. Later (a carefree later) we're still happily languorous. Hungry now, but the comfort of our room just being our room for a while is enough to keep me pinned to the bed.

I hear the car door slam first, then the kids. Their shrilling voices tell me they're still on a Grandma high. My Mum's pitch mirrors theirs, "Yes, yes!! We can tell Mummy what you've made".

Still star-fished and staring at the ceiling, I rise smiling. They burst through the door, kids roaring our names repeatedly whilst hunting us down. They find me and press me hard.

41

Mum holds up the homemade pizza and waves it in her hand. "Hungry love?"

After luxuriating in this slightly forgotten world, we orbit back to reality. It's come full circle – complete now you're all home.

Big Girls, Little Lies

Your stride seems longer, you're not galloping as
much, nor am I pigeon-stepping to the pace at which
you absorb the world.

You keep holding my hand (thankfully); I tell you
"Mine is what big girls are made of" so you squeeze it,
yearning for osmosis. A concept you don't yet
understand, or perhaps you do as you pull harder,
allow me this little lie, let me cling to you a little
longer.

Your hand in mine makes moments soft – softer than
the hollow at your collarbone, which, when tickled,
reveals your wide smile. A smile that holds the only
pearls left over from your infancy. Where you follow
I will lead, until those baby teeth (like you) push to
make space for more growth.

I'll tell you about the Tooth Fairy (see, a little lie).
I won't share that she's been visiting you nightly since
your birth.

I'll selfishly cry at a loss (that's no loss) then smile,
bittersweet with my own big girl teeth; I watch on as
you take a big bite at the world with yours.

Partners Prior To Parents

We're folding love like bedsheets
The damn corners don't always meet
But when they do it's worth the effort
I'm tangled up in the covers and
finally, it's with you
A susurrus of rising excitement spills
into our old, half-finished conversations
They're revived with speed and laughter
It's a mellifluous and contagious sound
that's been muted for too long
It's late and I should sleep
but I'll not abandon our time
As parents, it's too often left to cascade
down the priority list,
I'll try hard, try hard not to ever abandon us

I've Just Had A Baby (after Annie Ridout)

I'd just had a baby and only then did they share
their real birth stories
<insert shocked face and unspoken swear words>.

I had been told not to worry, as hundreds and
thousands before me had done it; "Do not fear dear"
the parting gift at my late summer baby shower.

Now he's in my arms we finally stand on relatable
ground, yet I'm still trying to swim, and I've never
really been a strong swimmer have I.

All I see is that red river flowing uncontrollably, I'm
bobbing, just reaching the surface, trying to breathe
out a Mother… "You'll be fine, you'll recover."

Half Term

Monday morning excitement
Coffee cup requirement
Spooky Halloween crafts
My poetry left in drafts
Visits to the park
Films in the dark
Amazon box boats
Test if it floats
Long autumn walks
Long Granny talks
Activity day outing
Gift shop shouting
Siblings squabble
Mum due a wobble
Repeat Paw Patrol
Test Mum's control
Playmobil creations
Video-call relations
Kitchen cake baking
Living room mess making
Speedy scooter rides
Big swing and slides
Build a blanket den
Snacks – what again?!!
Save bread for the duck
Did Mum whisper fu*k?
Dad's conference call
Ruined by us all

I'm Selling The Pram

The words stung on the edge of my tongue.
"Ok great, that will free up some space," he replied.
Is that it?
"Space in the boot or under the stairs."
That's it?!!
Yes, I know this is overly unfair as I've been battling
most of this privately –
But that decision took me months,
And he's seemingly found a more convenient space
for the Christmas tree in seconds.
I'm done, we're done, no more babies.
No more folding, clipping or nipping my finger.
No more awful coffee cup holder that did a terrible
job of containing the coffee in my cup
(its only job I might add!).
I pine over the rhythmic bumping of wheels, swirling
over the pavement cracks that soothed you to sleep,
The day we turned you forward to face the world,
pushing you proudly with my bouncing show-off strides.
You waved adorably to passers-by, like you were in
your own pageant show.
Then when your sister came along 18 months later,
we upgraded to an inline double.
Ohhh double fancy, double seats, double trouble,
double the adventures.
I paraded my mini double-decker like a beaming bus
driver – you know, the one who would let you off if
you forgot your fare, yeah that one.

It's been parked up redundant for quite some time,
Brought out for the odd occasion to support your tired
starting-school legs.
You tell me you don't need buckling in anymore.
I've argued with, cried about, contained, ignored and
now finally answered that soft voice and phantom
umbilical cord tug:

"Shall we have another baby?"

I suppose I too should find happiness in the hoover
having a permanent home.

Other than the acceptance of "We're done," it's the
deafening realisation:

"But what if I'm not good at anything else anymore?"

Stay At Home Mum

What's next? they ask…
I've not thought about it really.
Oh, Lady of Leisure?
This quickly makes me queasy.

I scramble for answers
To halt the fear that's growing.
I simply don't have one,
My panic's visibly showing.

What's your plan for a "real" job?
What about your old place?
What's not real about my current one?
I push back desperate for space.

Embossed hard in my thoughts,
The question, it shouts out,
Over analysing my significance,
Force feeding my self-doubt.

The answer's stuck in my throat like peanut butter.
Feeling lost in this mess of validation clutter:
I'm a Stay At Home Mum, I softly mutter.
(Is this not enough? I rhetorically utter.)

20/20 (Vision)

Please lend me your eyes
I want to see what you dream
Fear or fantasy

Please lend me your eyes
Crisp innocence and kind heart
Beautifully clear

Please lend me your eyes
Confidence and clarity
A focus on fun

Please lend me your eyes
They grew bright inside me
But through you, I now see

What Are You Wearing Around Your Neck?

Arms
Small arms
Small but make me big arms
I play dot-to-dot with her moles. . .
Stopping at each one as I map out her beauty
She finds mine and the hereditary constellation
becomes a game between us
I'm blessed to wear both sets of pigmentation
pearls today

Adulting

It's been over 16 years since I legally became an adult.
So why do I still endure growing pains?
I thought I left them in my adolescence,
along with the catalogue of other prior pain.

I stand on these aching limbs, shepherd to my own flock.
They gladly follow me (most of the time, and other
times they follow too much).
Never alone, yet I can't avoid the moments of feeling

abandoned.

Like I'm destined for the lost-and-found box,
Where I'm picked up, shaken down and even pulled
inside out –
Only to be left again, under the weight, under the
weight of, well, everything… adult.

But I still call my own Mum for so much.
Can I cook this from frozen?
Seems to be a popular one.
I call to chat. Sometimes we belly laugh
and sometimes I call to just cry.

She says, "You can always come home for a holiday
you know". My heart immediately and immaturely
sinks, wishing her sentence had omitted the "for a
holiday you know".

She leaves me with sound advice and tells me I'm doing a fabulous job. I'll ignore it, and call to discuss it all over again next week.

Yes. Mother knows best. But which one?

Footprints

Dear Daughter step into my shoes
Safe with their buckled fastenings
I hope I'm providing comfort and support
The paths we take and who we walk with aren't
by chance
It's choice
I hope I'm choosing wisely
We're laying foundations with fierce affection
My concrete hopes and dreams pour in
Set and sealed with your blossoming spirit
One day I'll watch you craft architecture
that proudly sits on top of what we started
Remember you have a choice and the
power to design buildings how you wish
With bricks of your significance
My shoes don't fit you but that doesn't stop you
wearing them
Test them out, tip toe on what you like and kick
off what you don't
You ride on my feet in our kitchen slow dance
You're stepping in time to the growing tune of
magnificence
I hum hopes of what you will become
With your own choices
Step inside mine, then make your own footprints

Cancelled Due To Covid

Summer chat
Simply that
No preparation
Or expectation
Words heard
Teas stirred
Parent groans
Partner moans
Kids hiding
Mums residing
Shared cake
Needed break
Belly laughter
Smiles after
Chatty bliss
This I miss

Daddy And Me

The nickname that you gave me
which nobody else gets,
Our rough-and-tumble play fights
and our silly-billy bets.

Our endless competitions
1
2
3
The smile that you give me
is my winner's trophy.

At least four more sweets
than Mummy ever gives.
Our sugarcoated secret
that she will sure forgive.

Goody vs baddy battles
I don't like to lose,
Momentary enemies –
Settled calling truce.

Bedtime story snuggles
dreams sketched out for the night
Daddy-and-me moments –
tomorrow we'll continue to write.

RAGE

I'VE CHOPPED VEGETABLES SO SMALL
THEY'RE FIT FOR A SYLVANIAN FAMILY.
STIRRED INTO THE SAUCE, THEY HIDE
FROM MINE.
INSTANT SQUAWKS OF DISGUST AND
REFUSAL.
WORDS OF ENCOURAGEMENT I SERENADE,
ACT OUT A CHEERY DISPOSITION CHARADE.
HER ACTING IS BETTER THAN MINE.
SHE GAGS LIKE IT'S A BUSHTUCKER TRIAL.
DAD HAS SUGGESTIONS.
STOP.
"PUDDING IS YOUR PRIZE."
JUST STOP.
I POUND MY FIST ON OUR TIRED TABLE
UNDERESTIMATING MY STRENGTH, OR WAS
IT FED BY MY PIT OF ANGER?
IT THROBS, AS DO I FOR SOME DAMN
APPRECIATION.
I'M FRANTICALLY CRUMB-CLEANING IN AN
ATTEMPT AT DISTRACTION – SEE I'M
REALLY TRYING.
I CAN'T CONTAIN IT MUCH MORE.
DAD SUGGESTS AGAIN.
TWO FINGERS I HOLD UP LIKE I'M TRYING
TO PAUSE HIM.

I STARE HARD AT MY PLATE.
SO HARD.
I FANTASISE ABOUT SHOOTING RED LASER
BEAMS FROM MY EYES THAT DETACH ME
FROM THIS DINING DISASTER.
HIS FORK TEETERING ON THE EDGE OF
THE TABLE.
I WATCH IT TOY WITH ME,
IS IT MOCKING ME?
AS I TOO AM SWINGING, TRYING TO FIND
STEADY GROUND.

OF COURSE,
IT FALLS.

I HAD SAID SO.

ITS DULL DING ON A STICKY FLOOR
IS THE FINAL STRAW.
I RISE SHARPLY.
THE RAGE MAKES ME FLEE.

Kitchen Bangs

Moody day
No progress day
Go the heck away day
I want a brand spanking new kitchen someday
But not soft-close drawers; how will I slam them to say
NOT TODAY?!!

Trike To Bike

Sore pedal-bashed shins
Even I ached wanting to scoop you up
Five-year-old frustration
Apparently, it's all my fault
Knee kisses are Mum's
magical medical marvel
Let's go again
Ready
Steady
Pedal
Don't stop, don't stop!
His rosy-cheeked face broke
out in smiles of amazement
I'm doing it, I'm doing it!
His personal cheerleaders,
we were loud in supportive song
We didn't pause or care to think who else heard
Just as long as he did

ii.   Motherhood Is...

longing for a quiet moment, some alone time,
yet when I get it, I'm still surrounded by noise
(just this time it's the deafening thrum of guilt)

Unearthed

My priorities were left somewhere, maybe they're
piled up high in the barely-touched book pile.

I pick them up briefly, only to put them away again as
my concentration is flagging or I'm needed elsewhere.

Perhaps they're gathering dust with the never-ending
dining table clutter. We push them around, out of the
way, out of reach, out of sight. They're rarely picked
up and dealt with fully, left dwindling, dissolving,
denied of any dedication,

derelict.

Someone handed me a shovel, told me to dig;
I've seen my value, my worth. I will prioritise the
gardening again, I'll dig deeper, plant more seeds,
nurture, care for and unearth what's blooming
within me…

Climb

As I run towards unknown endings,
blind faith beckons as my North Star.
Self-doubt steps alongside, but
I walk on, bold and brave.
When I was last lost,
benevolent
hearts lifted
me to
climb.

Water

I promised myself I'd consume eight glasses of water today and I've only managed two. The first, I clumsily knocked over (still counting it). The other, split between myself and the neglected houseplants. I seem to always catch ~~myself~~ them right before that point of no return. Lazily lucky or carelessly caring, I'm not sure. God knows when I last took the time to study ~~myself~~ my windowsill pretties or care for ~~myself~~ them fully.

Cardboard Hearts

Blast off in our handmade rocket
The rug cushions our moon landing
Your youthful imagination is contagious
I quickly lose gravity
Hotels, towering castles
Base camps when we're exploring
Steam trains chug along
Stopping at dreamt-up destinations –
The ticket price extortionate!
I willingly pay the fare for this journey
Hospital beds for teddies that need patching up
You nurse them back to good health
Even outside this fantasy world you've healed me too
I can't wait for the next adventure
Lead me with your vivid imagination
Whilst I collect these cardboard hearts

New Kind Of Drunk

From tipsy twenties
Now we watch our children play
Drunk on their laughter

Dedicated to our friends J & P and their darling daughters.
Getting to raise children at the same time as your friends is a
beautiful gift.

Illustrator – Rachel Dickens
@lollysnow

Rainbows

We paint rainbows with fierce affection
A deluge full of hope for the good old days is
intensified with each stroke
Holding back tears, I let the paint do the crying
Every sweeping brush marks a longing to hear
familiar voices and their stories untold
A bleeding spectrum forms an arched entrance,
open and ready to welcome a brighter day
The colours hold each other up
Like us, they're stronger together
And just like the rain, I remind myself;
this too shall pass

Rookie

Over plan
Over pack
Won't do this
Won't do that
Got it sussed
No way fussed
Baby's here
I disappear

Of All The Things I Left Behind

Of course, I expected change, we couldn't do it **all** could we… could we? **The** call to sacrifice **things** that we loved was willingly accepted, so we made space, we changed pace, **I** smiled and cried with this same face, yet I just struggled to recognise myself, and, even now, I still search for who I **left behind**.

Music Be Medicine

It's 3am
You're burning up
Through tears you ask
me to sing our song

You need magic pink medicine?
You nod shyly, "Mummy sing again"

Is that better now?
Big brown puppy dog eyes ask
"Just one more song mama?"

What's In A Name?

We took months writing a list of names, removing any should someone mention they knew one who was a "bad egg".

Your Dad made the final choice; my concrete certainty in him making caring choices for you was present from day one.

Your surname, carried from Afghanistan to India, strapped to the backs of Mothers as they navigated the unknown, harvested in each grain of rice that they grew, for the you they never knew.

Now you answer to multiple nicknames, endearing words that we've plucked from moments of joy and laughter, gracing us with you in all we see and do.

Wiping

I wipe
butts, cuts,
tears from fears,
20 sticky fingers and
a stain that really lingers,
doors, floors whilst on all fours
chins, grins and bruised little shins
dropped chicken dinners, no tea-time winners
brows hearing fables as heads I gladly cradle

Wiping so hard, have I removed all trace of my
former self?

Look Up

Your lip quivers first
Your eyes dart from
me to the floor then
back to look up again
Child, I see you're hurting
Hurts twice, as I try to absorb it
Sitting tight on my chest
I could fold in on myself
with this rush of protection
Pulling you in harder expels
some pain and steadies me
You collapse in and mould
to my chest, your tears flow
and take rest on my shoulder
Wet polka dots spread over my
shirt, the shapeless cotton and
familiar smell comforts me too
As I continually learn to
mother you

Mummified

Mummy can you lie down here?
Keep really still
Close your eyes too
Ok, I'll now take out your organs
I'll give you your heart back
Your brain is next
This comes out through your nose
Now I'll wrap you up
Sprinkle on some salt and spices
Don't move Mummy
Keep really, really still

It might sound painful
But it's my favourite game yet
Mummy being mummified
What a welcome rest

This Way Friend

I watched on from the crossroads
Terrain inviting yet the path unknown
Others kept joining the route
With each step they strangely grew taller
Each stride stronger, strangers, yet they had
arrived all humming the same song
It sounded familiar, so very familiar
Just when I placed my first step
Hesitation radiated up through me
Stopped just as quickly when it clashed with comfort
She had placed one hand on my shoulder and with
the other she was pointing to the sign
We walked on sharing stories of our differing but
relatable worlds
When we turned the corner
I was confronted with the most magnificent mosaic
My eyes darted back and forth in awe of the creation
The humming had turned into full song
Shards of many shapes slotted together like they had
been cut from the same stone
Yet each piece was uniquely painted
Together, it shone harmoniously
She pointed to a space
Told me to add in my own tile
That's when the lyrics hit me

Rebuild Me

ruins
fallen, crumbled
memory mounds, trace
in dust "I'm not
ruined"

collect
your debris,
tears in abundance
set cement, you can
rebuild

Guilt

It's Mother's Day I tell them
So I sip fresh coffee alone
Swallowing guilt again
Just today it's piping hot

Illustrator – Debbie Brown

Without Using The Word – Tell Me You're A Mother

I'm one side of quotation marks,
waiting for the pair to be complete
anywhere between 10pm and 3am.

Tiny camouflaged men are left to hide in
my carpet, a surprise attack, shot in the
piggy who should have gone to market.

Evolved; medicinal lips wick away
pain in an instant, octopus limbs carry
more than I ever thought imaginable.

Grown, stretched and torn
(physically and mentally) yet I'm reminded
daily that I've also been truly blessed.

Nostalgia Stage Call

Steamrolled daily by your emerging talents
Since birth, it's been my job to coach you
One day you'll play lead
Your very own life production
Unconsciously in rehearsal
No need to audition
Acts played out in front of me
Motherhood matinee
Casting your own cast
You're growing up too fast
Momentarily slide into my private box
You're in crisp sharp focus
Spotlight is soft
The auditorium snaps me back with roars
of ferocious approval
I also applaud you, always
Can I extend the intermission and be
delighted by your immaturity a little longer?
I know this confirms your growth
Dependency swapped for independent stage direction
Could the stage momentarily
please
stand
still
I'll be lovingly waiting for what's to come in your
encore

Mother The Mother

I ran away fast from its humble hometown shuffle,
I wanted more, this 17-year-old knew better, and the
big city called me south.

The lights were bright and always left on here – how
extravagant! Had Mum seen she would have been
moaning at how steep the electricity bills would be.

The sound of seagulls had been swapped for birds of
roaring metal flying back and forth overhead. The
scent of sea salt now absent, only an artificial trace of
it left, holding onto waves made in my hair.

Heading due north, I'm now a visitor in my
hometown. And the homesickness, it's more than just
nausea – it burns.

See, this Mother needs mothering too. But I accept
that a hug and a perfect dippy egg in my 1996 'Only
Smarties have the answer' egg cup four times a year
will have to do.

Resolutions

I start jotting them down, they always end up like a
reverse shopping list, noting all the food I plan to cut
out, insert an ideal image of what I think I should look
like, add in an end goal and deadline, usually some
material gratification of a trip to the shops where I'm
to buy clothes three sizes smaller than my current size,
I underline it hard three times, like I'm angry before I
even succumb to defeat, I've failed consecutively, year
on year, yes, on the resolution, but even more so as a
role model and as a Mother to my dear daughter...

My next year's resolution:

I
promise
to
never
make
such
damaging
shopping
lists
again.

iii.   Motherhood Is…

pencil lines dated on the door frame, no amount of erasing can prevent bittersweet change becoming a permanent feature

Cherish

I mean you no harm
When I fold you up small
Placed into my pocket
Keep safe keepsake
I fear this a selfish hold
So I bring you out
Show you the sun
Unfold your broken wings
My hands the nest
Worried of a fall
But if it's flight you want
I won't crush you anymore

Illustrator – Rebecca Green
@herworldofdiscovery

Five

When did that happen?
Where did time go?
You came home so tiny
And defenceless you know

We used to sleep softly
During many a nap
And enjoy baby classes
Where you sat on my lap

Picnics and play dates
With our new parent friends
Nappies and muslins
With fun to no end

Five you say?
Are you really sure?
Feels like only yesterday
You took first steps on this floor

Then came the tantrums
Your mischievous ways
Toddling around
Whilst learning through play

Nursery you took to
With your energy and smile
I missed you like crazy
I cried for a while

Then it was school
That you took in your stride
Making new friendships
Filling me with pride

Happy birthday darling
Enjoy, feel alive!
You've mastered age four
Now good luck being five

Ballerina

Her 3-year-old sweet sharp intake
A birthday gift to hold any treasure
"It's mine?" she gasps

After celebrating all day, she tires early
I lay my treasure down to sleep
"She's mine!" I gasp

A melodic Mother's love
I'm twirling on tiptoes
Dancing in delight to it

Treats

It's exhausting a lot of the time
Moments of defeat can be deafening
But when the triumphs hit it's so worth it
I reward you with stickers, you run to place them on
the front of the fridge
I too take my reward
Firstly, I smile proudly at the spray of stars,
thumbs-ups and smiley faces
Secondly, I open the door and grab the chilled
Chablis and chocolate ganache
In the cold blue glare, I breathe out happy

Me Time

I just wanted a little me time
I've re-read this paragraph four times
What is it now!?
I just wanted a little me time
I hear your tiny steps back out on the landing
My eyes already rolling
I just wanted a little me time
You reappear with a new and imaginative request
I JUST WANTED A LITTLE ME TIME
I launch the book into my duvet
MY duvet!
MY book!
I just wanted a litt...
Your sad dark eyes cut me
My brewing anger shrinks
I laugh nervously
I'm instantly heavy with guilt
Your shuffling feet
Tiny hands twist and twirl into your pyjamas
Your painted pink toes now pressed hard into the
bedroom carpet
What is it, sweetheart?
You stutter softly
Mu...Mummy
You just wanted a little cuddle
I just wanted a little me time
But so did you

You Are Enough

"When I'm bigger Mummy,
I want to be just like you."

I tell her: "But you, darling,
are so much more."

As the words leave my lips
I'm reminded, learning to love myself
will show her she is enough.

A real-life conversation with my daughter.

Dedicated to Ona, who selflessly made me see and believe that
this was true, thank you.

Guiding Hands

I read her upturned palm
Unique pathways paved
Yet we've walked streets
petaled with parallel pain
She tells me to clasp on tight,
as there are also fortunes to behold

Illustrator – Rebecca Green
@herworldofdiscovery

Out

Will I have to retrain myself to go outside? I mean,
beyond the basics of walking one foot in front of the
other. I tell others I'm longing to go out, but
I've noticed a growing comfort and feeling of safety
inside these walls…

I must remind myself of all the things I miss out there:

The quick reactive nip to the shop without concern
or caution.

Play dates indoors, we just show up and buy a ticket
(no pre-booked time slot).

< Freedom >

The warmth of the sun on a late June morning, how it
hugs my bare shoulders as we step outside.
We've excitedly packed picnics to share with our
friends, outside we're passing food to each other,
loving hands that accidentally touch without snapping
back with a fretful apology, just loving hands.

< Touch >

At the farmers' market we join the growing crowd, magnetised by the buzzing chatter, the lure of unknown surprises behind the sea of people, and the satisfaction of consuming tasty samples of locally-grown goodies.

< Community >

My friend offers me a sip of her strawberry-infused rum punch at the summer festival. I pick up my nephew when he trips over and grazes his knee.

< Unconscious love >

Will I step out without question again?
Too outrageous?
Or am I out of my mind?

iv.   Motherhood Is…

becoming a private translator
for a rather demanding boss,
but son I get you, always

Silent Nights

I tuck your walnut silk ribbons behind your ear,
making sure you can hear my forty-wink wishes.
I hope you're dreaming in a world of your design.

Are you running through powder-pink fields,
swept with candy floss for miles?
Or are you swimming across an ice-cream lake,
debris swapped for rum 'n' raisin?

Silent beds make my apologies louder; can you feel
my quiet kiss rest upon your peached percale skin?
Are you asleep or sweetly pretending?
And do you forgive me?

Bond

Bo(rn into a love without e)**nd**

Illustrator – Patricia Galligan
@patriciagalliganart

Let Her Dream

Focus
Pick your vocation
Stay on track
Know your destination

Keep within the lines
No room for error
Parental pressure
Hurricane terror

She's changed her mind
She yearns for something new
She needs support and
validation from you

Stop, watch and see her
(Perhaps for the first time)
Shackled to your wishes
What is her crime?

Discovering herself
Hear her cry
Don't steal this moment
Instead watch her fly

Let her dream
Ambitions – her own
Your new dream is to
watch how she grows

Both Finally Asleep

Asleep
At last
Synchronised soft slumber
Don't wake yet
Keep dreaming

Illustrator – Debbie Brown

Undone

Zip
Often too open and
occasionally embarrassed

Buttons
Undone, in a silk shirt seduction?
No, just absent minded

Biscuit Jar
Attempting more sweet than stale,
but sometimes empty

Laces
Strong double knots slip to
trailing, tired and tangled

Hair
Could spend more time on it,
wanting it to grow

Belt
Flexible and adaptive,
also holding a lot up

ode to my notes app

thank you for holding my frantic finger fury, never a
hint of judgement, and my goodness, thank you for
the much-needed solace in silence you always offer

you listen so well, I'm grateful for the spell-check and
even more so the mental health check, catching my
reflection upon your unassuming glass glare

laughter and smiles as my pearls beam with nostalgia,
to times recalling trauma, you collect free-falling tears,
cradling me and my cathartic creativity

some shared for the world to see, others float to the
cloud –
saved for only you and I

More Than Mummy Mates

Our October babies' laughter the backing track to
our day. We sang over it. Our lyrics all catch-up
stories played out in double speed, yet fully heard.

Yellow bruises are the oldest. We've shared and
healed from so many. Together again, we collectively
begin to recover… as we thaw out from
enforced hibernation.

Looking around it was a wash of denim. We sat apart,
desperate to hug but grateful; we settled on gusts of
April kisses caught on the wind.

It was all Mum genes in our Mom jeans, fitting just as
it always had – a little leftover houmous inviting us to
come back and dip into all of this again once more.

Pick A Number

As a child I'd get momentarily lost in my own world, making origami paper fortune tellers. I'd fold the paper at the exact middle of the page, believing precision and structural perfection would add to their accuracy, therefore swaying any luck.

Now, as an adult I'd tell her... I see your hope, hold onto that. But life won't always fold how you want it. Tear off the crap much sooner; make paper planes instead kid,

go see where they fly on their own.

Thank you to…

My friends and family – It was so scary initially sharing my poetry with you. I shouldn't have worried, you've been nothing but supportive and encouraging throughout.

Zachary and Jessie – If you ever read this collection, I hope you feel my love through each and every word. When I was tested or struggling, my love and care for you was never in question. You are the anchors who hold me steady in any storm. I'm so proud of you both and who you are blossoming into.

Sanjay – If you say you're married "to a poet and you didn't know it" one more time, I'll... still be smiling. Thank you for listening and believing in me.

Illustrators: Debbie Brown (my Aunt), Rebecca Green, Rachel Dickens and Patricia Galligan – Your talent leaves me in awe; what a gift you all have. I'm so grateful that your images are in this collection. Truly honoured.

Proof-reader: Catherine Hamilton – Thank you for your eyes and ears (not just with this project but also within a new-found friendship). Also, many thanks to the other kind people who generously offered their time to proofread my work.

Editor: Philippa Davies (@philippa_davies_books)

1. I'm blessed to have you as an amazing friend in real life; you've been with me for my entire motherhood journey and beyond.
2. I couldn't afford your full professional fees, so I'm just going to refer you back to point 1.
3. Love always.

(If you're looking for a book to keep the little ones entertained while you read this one, please do check out Smidge and the Mountain MoOobles – which Philippa wrote and illustrated during the first lockdown. Zachary and Jessie are big fans.)

To the poetry community – A huge thank you for your kind comments, feedback and critique.
Thank you also for sharing your own stunning words; what an unbelievably talented bunch you all are.

There are a few of you who I've made a deeper connection with. Forgive me for not naming you all individually, but I hope you know who you are and have felt the friendship and love reciprocated.
Your chat, banter and often more personal words have felt like a much-needed hug over the strange year we've had – especially as I started pushing my poetry out to the world.

The Mum Poem Press – I can't thank you enough. You were there with open arms at exactly the right time. Your encouragement, motivation and momentum has been so needed. Through your group I've met so many amazing and inspiring people.

Sarah Parrott (@writesparks) – Thank you for your fabulous creative writing course. Ideal for Mothers who want to start writing about their journey, and all at their own pace – I highly recommend it. (You were also the first person to publish one of my poems. Seeing "Dear Government" featured in the amazing Dear 2020 Project Zine was a moment of recognition and validation that I will never forget.)

Bloodmoon Journal – Such a welcoming and supportive community. Thank you for the fabulous educational tools and for helping to enable my continued growth and development. What a brilliantly joyous journey.

Nikki Dudley (@mumwrite) – Huge thanks for your fabulous courses aimed at Mums who want to write, as well as the super supportive community you've created for us to join.

Finally, thank you to you. If you've kindly purchased a copy of this collection, thank you so very much. I hope you've enjoyed reading it as much as I enjoyed writing it.

@new_stanza

Those of you who follow me on social media will know I'm a big fan of **poetry prompts**. They have provided me with lots of writing inspiration, for which I am truly grateful (especially during those dry spells of writer's block). I also love reading other writers' responses to prompts – always beautifully surprised by how people interpret them so differently.

As my final thank you, here are some poetry prompts that I hope inspire you to write.

If you would like to share your responses, please do use **#NewStanzaBookPrompts** to help me find them online.

- Stumbling through
- Park life
- Dot to dot
- On your bike
- Are you sleeping?
- Amber afternoons
- Leftovers
- The first time
- Colours of my/their childhood
- Footprints of forgiveness

Praise For This Collection

"No Walk In The Park is a wonderfully varied collection that celebrates motherhood without sugar coating it. At times wry and warm, at others raw and vulnerable, Jemma Chawla's work never fails to be unflinchingly honest. I found myself nodding along emphatically with her at so many points during this book – it's a vivid, often funny and at times painfully true exploration of the rollercoaster of early parenthood that would make a fabulous gift for anyone embarking on the same journey."
JEN FEROZE
Author of "The Colour of Hope"

"Vulnerable, tender and oh-so-relatable.
A validating, timeless and beautiful read for mothers everywhere."
KAREN MCMILLAN
Author of "Mother Truths" and "Lessons"

"This debut collection of poetry on early motherhood can only be described as an electrifying, pulsating and riveting read. The author cleverly plays with various poetic forms while also capturing the multi-faceted experiences of being a parent. These honest narratives and conversations are so needed right now. The pandemic has allowed us all a level of introspection and helped enable powerful new female voices such as these to emerge."
ONAJITE CLARKE
Blogger, Activist, Coach and
Author of "The Secrets of my Ukulele"

"I have worked with professional writers (across multiple genres) for the past 17 years – but very few have caught my attention like Jemma. She has a natural flair for capturing the beautiful details of life in her poetry, particularly when it comes to motherhood and being a woman. Her words often dance playfully across the page...At times, they strike a deeper chord, cutting to the very core of what it means to be vulnerable, lost, angry or alone. In every instance, they are a joy to read. This is Jemma's first complete anthology – but I certainly hope it isn't her last."

PHILIPPA DAVIES
Creative Consultant, Copywriter, Editor and Children's Author/Illustrator

Printed in Great Britain
by Amazon

62014699R00066